SEVENTY
Times
SEVEN

Janice P. Dixon

Because There's More Publishing | Georgia

ISBN: 979-8-9921977-3-0 (Paperback)
ISBN: 979-8-9921977-2-3 (Hardcover)

Library of Congress Control Number: 2025903386

Printed in the United States of America.

Published by:
Because There's More Publishing LLC
PO Box 390163
Snellville, GA 30039
becausetheresmorepublishing.com

I dedicate this book to our Lord and Savior, Jesus Christ. If it weren't for His unfailing love, I would not be here, and you would not have this book in your hands.

I am forever grateful.

CONTENTS

SEVENTY TIMES SEVEN
Introduction

Life is funny sometimes. It's a journey filled with unexpected and challenging moments, good and bad. At times, these challenges can weigh on us, leaving our souls tired and damaged from the hurt and disappointment. When life gets hard, it's easy to grow weary, frustrated, and even bitter. But there's something crucial I've learned. Starting with, you have to be careful not to let bitterness and unforgiveness take root and take over your heart. This is not an easy task, trust me. I had to be intentional and work hard to keep my heart in the right place. Secondly, I had to realize the act of forgiveness is at the heart of our own healing and freedom.

As human beings, we are made up of three parts – our spirit, our body, and our soul. Let's take a closer look at the soul. The Merriam Webster dictionary defines the soul as "a person's total self, an active or essential part - the moral and emotional nature of human beings." It is the soul that encompasses our mind, will, and emotions. It holds our deepest pains and our greatest joys. I like to look at it as our thinker and feeler.

Sometimes, you go through so much for so long, you begin to dread what's coming next.

I don't think you ever fully get over some things. It just becomes more manageable. You learn to function in everyday life again, and in time, choose to move forward. At some point, you have to protect yourself and living in a toxic environment is so unhealthy. It's a hard decision, but you have to move on no matter how bad it hurts. I know it's painful, but it's painful to stay in it too. Holding on to the pain only keeps you stuck.

I don't care how down you think you are, there is nothing too deep or bad that God cannot pull you out of, if you let Him. However, to be free, you must forgive. That's the only way you'll truly move forward. You see, forgiveness is not about letting others off the hook - it's about freeing yourself from the pain of bitterness and resentment.

"Resentment is like drinking poison and then hoping it will kill your enemies."
Nelson Mandela

When you've been in a difficult situation for a long time, it's easy to run in the opposite direction once you're free, or even procrastinate or withdraw because the pressure has been lifted.

Someone once asked me how I would describe my life. I said it felt like holding a large stack of papers organized in alphabetical order. Then, all of a sudden, a huge gust of wind blew them out of my hands. As I struggled to get them back, the rug was snatched from underneath me. In that moment, everything changed, and life as I knew it was no longer the same. So now, I'm working with what's left to rebuild, because some of those papers were never recovered. They were lost forever.

Life isn't fair. No matter how bad you wished it was different, it's not. I'm sharing this because you must keep fighting to survive and move forward. That's the only way you're going to get through it. Even if you could go back, there might not be anything worth returning to. So, keep pushing forward. That's what I had to do. I had to learn to begin again - over and over - until I found peace and progress that allowed me to exhale. It might be slow, but it's still a step in the right direction. Learn how to appreciate and celebrate the small victories. Be proud of yourself for being strong and standing up to life.

I used to hear the phrase "take it day by day," but for me, it was "if I can just make it to the next moment." Of course, I didn't know what was going to happen or what the rest of the day or night would be like. I constantly lived in fear of what might hit me or what was coming my way, and all I could do was focus on the now and deal with it as it presented itself to me, the best I knew how at the time.

I'm still learning. I'm learning to pace myself, to not grab more than I can handle. I'm learning that, in order to reach where I'm supposed to be in life, I need to separate myself from some things and certain people. Only then can I see and hear clearly enough to move to the next level.

This is My Story

I've experienced a broken heart, sickness of a loved one, pain, chaos, frustration, loneliness, betrayal, and almost unbearable grief. I wrote this book because sometimes - you can't retreat. You have to keep going, there's no looking back.

I remember when...

I remember when we used to love each other, and
we were brave, young, and smart.

Brave enough to say "I do."
We faced a future together; we had plans and were
so excited about the new adventure ahead.
We were partners and a team.

Somehow, we lost our footing, and at some point,
we didn't catch each other.

What happened?

I remember when I thought you loved me.
I remember when we loved each other.

CHAPTER 1
Starting Over

It took me a long time to write this book. I procrastinated because it triggered painful memories. Some things I don't remember, but I do remember fighting to keep my faith in God, believing for the very best, even when the very best was not happening. For the longest time, I thought maybe, just maybe, things would change and I could be happy. I believed that if I had enough faith to trust God, He would turn things around. But when that didn't happen, and so much time had passed, I became discouraged. I couldn't understand why it was taking so long for things to go right, if I was doing everything I thought I was supposed to do according to my faith.

When things don't turn out the way we thought or wanted them to, we feel like we've failed. We get embarrassed and don't want people to know what we're going through. So, we try to fix it. But starting over doesn't come from fixing everything - it comes from letting go. Whether it's going through a divorce, losing a job, dealing with relationship problems, or realizing our children didn't turn out the way we hoped, the key is to surrender it to God.

If you're not careful, you'll start trying to figure it all out, which can lead to unnecessary frustration. So, go ahead and accept the apology you might never get and move on with your life. Trust me! Let it go! This goes for us too. Stop trying to figure out why you made that decision and beating yourself up about it.

> *Father, I pray for everyone reading this book right now. I lift them up before You and ask for Your grace in their lives. Please show them Your love in such a way that doubt has no place and they KNOW it's You. In Jesus' name, Amen!*

When you're in the middle of your struggle, this is when you start to wonder why things are happening and why it's taking so long to turn around. You frustrate yourself trying to figure it out, but starting over means you have to stop trying to control it all. Do yourself a favor: don't. Life can be challenging enough, so take it one day at a time. Do your best, stay hopeful, and trust the Lord.

I know for some, you might not quite know how to do that, but over time you will learn. I can't really explain it, but life has a way of showing you how to start over. You begin building that relationship with God as you go through challenges or situations. It's gradual and peaceful at the same time. Yes, you're still hurting most of the time, but that's the process of starting over. Just continue to trust Him. There's no other remedy.

There are times in our lives when we cause our own hardships, and even then, God is still there. Starting over doesn't mean you won't face consequences - it just means you don't stay stuck in regret. Be careful not to fall into self-pity or anger toward yourself. We all go through this. Whether it's personal, career-related, or business-related, almost everyone has to start over at some point in their life. But you can't live in regret - it doesn't help you move forward. You have to learn to move on, accept that life is full of new beginnings, and realize that sometimes we thought we were making the right decision. So, give yourself a break. Don't beat yourself up. Forgive yourself! It's going to be okay. Yes, you may have to walk through some consequences, but who doesn't? That's when we pray and ask the Lord for wisdom. Even in this, He helps us.

Starting over can be life-changing - like dealing with a disease or a child born outside of marriage. Whatever it is, you can't change the past, and nothing is too hard for the Lord. I'm going to say this a lot throughout this book: What else are you going to do anyway? There is no one else but HIM.

Here are a few tips that will save you a lot of heartache:

- Don't make life-changing decisions based on temporary feelings.
- Don't make emotional decisions. Every decision you make, you'll see it again. Whether you're excited or angry, try to wait and sleep on it. Calm down and think about it.
- Calculate the cost by weighing the pros and cons, then come back around to your decision. I used to tell my children that all the time since they were about six or seven years old. I hope they got it!

CHAPTER 2

Unnecessary Frustrations

As I mentioned before, don't try to figure it all out. You're probably not going to anyway. Some things are within your control, and some things aren't. Love, by its very nature, gives people the power to hurt you. It makes you vulnerable. Trying to understand why people do the things they do is exhausting. You can't figure people out - they're way too complicated. Their grievances or complaints, especially when they seem to have no reason, often make no sense. They come from a place of anger, vindictiveness, or pride and, sometimes, they're simply trying to hurt you. Honey, let it go!

So many people are bitter, angry, and hurt, and they take it out on you and others. Trying to figure them out only leads to frustration. And remember, we can't always say or do exactly what we want either. God is good to them just like He's good to us, even if we don't like it. The truth is, sometimes we're not so good ourselves. So, try to keep the balance. If you let pride creep in, you'll lose perspective, and you'll start judging others.

It's incredibly hard to accept the fact that you will never get an apology and still forgive someone for what they did to you - especially when you've been so good to them. It's confusing and painful. But again, don't try to figure it out. I know it's not a good feeling; it's a deep hurt that stays with you. If you need help navigating through it, get counseling. It's okay, really. Some people are just too toxic for you to maintain a healthy relationship with and, for your own sanity, you have to leave. Be free from this kind of hurt. Don't allow yourself to become angry and bitter like them - that only keeps the cycle of pain going.

Keep moving forward, even without closure, explanation, or understanding. Pain is real. It's not just physical where you may need to visit the doctor; it can be emotional too, and that might also require a visit to the doctor. There are different types of pain, but the one I want to talk about is long term – aka - chronic trauma, which is what I mostly experienced. Chronic pain or trauma is a type of post-traumatic stress where someone experiences repeated or prolonged exposure to stressful and harmful situations leading to severe disruptions in their mental, emotional, and/or physical wellbeing. This can lead to PTSD.

Those things that trigger past hurts can bring on emotional moments - floods of tears, anxiety, or panic attacks. I've experienced all of them. Living a life of trauma is brutal. If you feel like you need help, please get it. It's tough, and there's no shame in seeking support.

But here's the beautiful thing: God is so tender and loving. He knows what you're going through, and He can heal you from all of it. He will work through whoever He needs to, just to get to you. There is nothing He can't heal, even if the offense happened 30 years ago. He is our soul's keeper.

Psalm 121:7-8 KJV says, "The LORD shall preserve thee from all evil: He shall preserve thy soul. The LORD shall preserve thy going out and thy coming in from this time forth, and even forevermore."

Just breathe, take a deep breath, and exhale.

CHAPTER 3
My Broken Heart

There is a scripture in the Bible that says, "He heals the brokenhearted and binds their wounds" (Psalm 147:3 KJV). Another version of that scripture, the NLT translation, reads, "He heals the brokenhearted and bandages their wounds."

Where do I begin? I know what it feels like to have a broken heart, and I know many of you do as well. Sometimes, it feels like it's never going to stop hurting or you're never going to be happy again.

When I first saw this scripture, I didn't fully understand it. Sure, I grasped the words, but when it came to healing my own heart, it felt different - this was personal. The vision I had for my life was nothing remotely close to what my life was like. I don't know if you've ever felt that way, but I think many people can relate. Life didn't go the way we planned, envisioned, or wanted.

Over time, I began to understand what the scripture meant. It meant exercising faith in God, even while I was hurting. At that point, there was nothing else for me to do but trust Him. I had nothing left to lose. This was when I truly began building my relationship with Jesus. And I don't mean just going through the motions - attending church, giving tithes, and pretending to be happy while feeling crushed inside. I mean really building a connection with Him. I actually imagined Jesus bandaging my wounds and healing my heart. Every day, I would say out loud, "Lord, Your word says You heal the brokenhearted and bandage their wounds." In my mind, I pictured Him gently putting bandages on my emotional scars, just as we would for a child who's fallen and skinned their knee.

My life had reached a point where I was desperate. I had no solutions and nowhere else to turn. I remember saying out loud, "Okay, it's me and You, God." My back was against the wall, and there was no one else to help. I remember being so sad, and this sadness was rooted in love - a love that had been shattered.

Let's talk about love for a moment. What is love? 1 Corinthians 13:4-8 NIV tells us that love is patient and kind; it does not envy or boast; it is not proud. It does not insist on its own way; it does not dishonor others, it is not easily angered, it keeps no record of wrongs. It always protects, trusts, hopes, and perseveres. Love never fails. My interpretation - love is long and expensive. It requires a trust that's uncertain, making us vulnerable and open to hurt. Vulnerability is scary; it brings fear with it. We all want love, but we're often afraid of it. Sometimes we play with the idea of love, but we hesitate to let go and commit.

Love can make you do things you swore you'd never do, like ignoring red flags. To be honest, in the early stages of a relationship, that might not even be love - it could be your instinct warning you to be cautious. Other times, we're so eager to love or be loved that we overlook the warning signs until it's too late. By then, we might already be deeply involved, maybe with children, and we keep hoping they will change. We think if we remain faithful, pray about it, and believe, God will fix it.

Love can bring pain, and when your heart is broken, there's no surgery or medication that can heal it. That takes God.

The heart is an intricate organ. It is both strong and fragile. On one hand, it pumps blood to keep us alive physically, but on the other hand it is delicate, needing the protection of the rib cage and covering of your pericardium or fluid-filled sac. It can be tender and loving, yet also hard, cold, and uncaring. If we're not careful, we can become so numb to our feelings that we just go through the motions of life without truly living. The heart endures a lot, and while some people can take more than others, everyone has their limits.

My pastor once said, "the ear is in the center of the heart". Which means we hear with our hearts. If you take the word "**HEART**" the word "ear" really is in the center of the word "H**EAR**T". If you look at the word "heart" again, you'll see the word "**HEAR**T." What a coincidence! We actually do hear with our heart, because spoken words can be taken to heart whether they're good or bad. That is one of the complicated miracles God has placed in us. So, the heart is a physical part of our body, but a spiritual part of our soul. That's deep!

There's a scripture that says, "Guard your heart, for out of it flow the issues of life." Think about that for a moment. What does that really mean? I believe "the issues of life" means the stuff that happens and how we feel about them. That goes back to me talking about the vulnerability and the hurts and joys that life can bring. It's interesting that it says "guard it." When we guard something, we're protecting it, right? So, God knew that we'd have to be careful with it. Unfortunately, sometimes we end up as collateral damage.

It also means that life's experiences - both the joys and the hurts - stem from the heart. And when the Bible tells us to guard it, God is warning us to protect it, knowing how fragile it is. Just as our ribcage protects our physical heart, we must protect our emotional heart too. Tears are sometimes a way of releasing those life issues, a cleansing of sorts. Lord knows I've cried my share of tears. It's okay to cry; it's good for the soul. Just let it go.

But what if you don't get what you prayed for, even when the Bible says you should? What if the healing or miracle doesn't come? These are difficult questions that so many of us ask. How can a loving God allow bad things to happen to good people, especially to the defenseless, like children? These are hard questions, and I don't claim to have all the answers. But I do know that God is love.

Think about it like this: if you have someone you love deeply, you'd do anything for them, right? But what if, one day, something terrible happens to them, and there's nothing you can do about it? Are you responsible for it? No. In the same way, I believe God is not responsible for every bad thing that happens in this world. Life happens, and sometimes it's painful. But that doesn't mean God doesn't love us or that He caused the hurt. Just like you wouldn't be blamed for something bad happening to a loved one, neither should God.

Now, try explaining that to a child. I had to do that. One day, my oldest son, who was 9 at the time, asked me, "Mommy, why isn't Jesus helping Daddy? Is it because of us?" My heart sank. It hurt so much to see his faith in God's word shaken. All I could say was, "Sometimes, things take longer than we want them to. We have to trust God, even when we don't understand."

CHAPTER 4
And Suddenly

Life has a way of throwing unexpected challenges at us. Sometimes these moments come with hurt and disappointment, while other times, they bring positive change and joy. Either way, they always seem to happen suddenly, catching us off guard. Most of the time, you have no control over them. They just happen.

I know what it feels like for your life to go from one thing to something else in an instant. These "And Suddenly" moments can bring heartbreak, sickness, pain, chaos, frustration, loneliness, humiliation, depression, betrayal, lies, and grief. When these disruptions occur, it can be difficult to regain your footing and focus. It's easy to get distracted, but you must keep going, even through the tears and the heartache. Fight to hold onto your peace. Fight!

At times, it feels like life is hitting you repeatedly, like a tsunami. In those moments, I've found myself thinking, "Can I just have a moment? Wait! Just give me a moment! I felt like I was being backed into a corner. I needed to catch my breath!"

That's when I learned that peace and boundaries are essential. You must find balance in your life.

Sometimes, the only way out is through, and establishing that balance helps you find your way back to a peaceful mind.

My "And Suddenly"

My husband was a healthy man - no illness, no warning signs. Then, one day, everything changed. He was at work when he suddenly fell. He said the room was spinning, and he lost his balance. They called paramedics, who took him to the nearest emergency room. After running numerous tests, the doctors couldn't find anything wrong. Still, they advised us to follow up with a neurologist, which we did.

After multiple doctor appointments and countless tests, everything appeared normal. We were so thankful. But as time went on, he began experiencing episodes of dizziness that left him completely drained. The doctors couldn't pinpoint the cause. They eventually gave him a diagnosis that seemed fitting, though it wasn't conclusive and wasn't confirmed by any of the tests. We were left dealing with the uncertainty.

As the years passed, his condition worsened, and the doctors were no closer to finding a proper diagnosis. We were in the emergency room every other day - literally. It got so bad that one day, after school, the crossing guard asked our son, "How's your dad doing?" The local firemen and paramedics all knew us. I hated it. I wanted him to be healed, to get our lives back. Our sons needed their father, and I needed my husband. But everything had changed. Our lives, as we knew them, were no more.

As his health declined, his spirit did too. Watching someone you love change, especially for the worse, is one of the hardest things to experience. I started to understand his anger - how a man like him, suddenly unable to provide for his family, must have felt. But in those moments, we only felt his wrath. I know he loved us, and we loved him, but everything was falling apart.

One day, exhausted and desperate, I prayed, Lord, please, what's wrong with him? I'm tired, and I don't know how much longer I can do this. I spent hours researching his symptoms online, trying to find answers. One day, I came across something that seemed to fit, something I hadn't heard of before.

The very next day, we found ourselves back in the ER. It was storming that day, a detail I'll never forget. As always, he had to go by ambulance because his episodes were so severe that I couldn't drive him. They gave him something to relax his muscles, and I followed behind after settling the kids. Once we got to the hospital, I showed the doctor what I had found online and asked if they could test for it. It took a few days, but finally, we had an answer. It was exactly what I thought. Who knew?

They started him on a treatment plan. Although he was never quite the same, we didn't have to live in the hospital anymore. He was finally stable, thank God. Physically stable, at least. But emotionally, he was still struggling. And I couldn't begin to imagine what all of this had done to him as a man.

I wish he could've seen how much I loved him, how I was willing to walk through anything by his side. This made me wonder if the Lord thinks the same about us. "Do they know how much I love them and will walk through anything with them?"

CHAPTER 5
The Fraternal Twins:
Trouble & Trauma

Trouble can come and go, but trauma is different. Trauma has a way of settling in and taking root. I want to be honest with you - I was so broken that I remember praying to the Lord one day, "Please don't let me die. Lord, please don't let me die." I didn't know if I would make it because I felt pushed to the point where I couldn't see a way out. There was no hope - or at least that's how it felt. My thoughts were consumed by my children and the people I loved. I didn't want to leave them. I wanted to see my sons grow up. I love life, and I didn't want to miss out on it. I was so overwhelmed!

But they that wait upon the Lord shall renew their strength; they shall mount up with wings as eagles; they shall run, and not be weary; and they shall walk, and not faint. Isaiah 40:31

When life doesn't turn out the way we thought or wanted, we often feel like we've failed. You can't fix every storm, and sometimes you don't even get a warning. It just happens. And many times, you don't have a choice because you can't control life itself - you can only control how you handle it. You have to learn how to get a healthy perspective and apply God's Word so you can navigate your way through it. Some things were so painful that they broke my heart in ways I can't even fully remember.

Everyone goes through storms, even when it seems like they don't. My life stayed in a bad place for what felt like an eternity and, looking back, I recognize it now as chronic trauma. But here I am - I survived. I'm not the same person I was, but I'm still here. I lived to see my sons grow up, and now they're fine young men. Thank you, Lord. I know I wouldn't have made it without You. You are my life, and I need You every day.

That was my journey, and I want you to know you can get here too. We're in this journey of life together, and I promise you, you're not alone, even when it feels like it.

I once heard a line in a movie that said, "God is like the wind - you can't see Him, but you can feel Him." I've never forgotten that. It took every ounce of strength I had to get back up. I felt defeated and alone, but I knew my God wouldn't forsake me. He wouldn't leave me in that dark place. He promised He wouldn't, and I believed Him at His Word. He made that promise to you too.

Hebrews 13:5 AMPC talks about us being content with what we have and not to be consumed with greed. There's another part of this scripture I want to focus on, and God Himself says, "I will not in any way fail you nor give you up nor leave you without support. [I will] not, [I will] not, [I will] not in any degree leave you helpless nor forsake nor let [you] down (relax My hold on you)! [Assuredly not!]

Whew! When I read this, it brought tears to my eyes. He says, "I will not" three times! Please know that He has you, and there's nothing and no one that can keep Him from getting to you.

You cannot allow others to make you feel guilty for their situations or the decisions they've made - no matter how much you love them. It's time to stand up for yourself. They defend their own choices, so why can't you? Don't let anyone misuse or abuse you just to prove that you love them. That doesn't prove anything. Maintain your peace and don't allow people to project their past traumas onto you either. Trust me, they will if you let them. Also, be free from people's opinions, because that kind of freedom is priceless.

Pray with me! Lord, teach us how to make quality decisions. Sometimes, we're still dealing with the consequences of choices we made years ago - friendships, relationships, situations we thought we could manage. I don't want to hinder my progress or jeopardize my future by going off course. I don't want to bring curses into my life through poor decisions.

Sometimes, we trust the wrong people, share our secrets, and open our hearts to them, only to later face the consequences of being transparent with the wrong person. That's one of the worst kinds of betrayal. Hurt people often make decisions that protect their feelings but not their future. However, hurt can't be the foundation for our lives. Bitterness and mood swings from unresolved pain don't just hurt us - they can damage the people around us. They cloud our judgment, making it impossible to see life clearly. We must deal with it or it will deal with us.

Again, we have to learn how to make good decisions, even while we're still hurting. Life can be both good and bad at the same time, and we must navigate it wisely.

CHAPTER 6
When There's No Closure

Every now and then you won't get closure, and that can be incredibly hard. What do you do when closure never comes? You have to trust God to help you push past it and move on. We often feel like we need closure, but the truth is, we can survive, live, and even find joy without it. What we really want is to understand—to know the "whys" and "why nots." In the end, we just want to make sense of what happened.

Why did this happen to me? Why didn't that person get healed when we prayed and believed God's Word? Why did they die? Why did my child turn out this way? Why did I lose my job? Why, why, why?

Trying to figure it all out will only frustrate you. I explain this in more detail in the chapter "Unnecessary Frustration." We all want closure, but we don't always get it. So, what do you do when it's not available? You have to learn to move on without it, because there may come a time when you have no choice. And really, what other option is there?

There are many things you're going to have to learn to do, even if you don't like it or don't have anyone to support you - and that's okay. The Lord is ALWAYS there, even when you don't feel His presence. To be honest, there will be times when you probably won't feel Him at all. But He's still there. Sometimes, there are no shortcuts. You have to take life as it comes, and you have to make up your mind to live and enjoy life anyway, even without closure.

The only way to truly enjoy life is to release everything and allow God to heal your heart. This isn't easy, and it won't feel good, but it's worth it. Think of it like anything else that's worth achieving - like getting healthy or making lifestyle changes you know you need to make in order to live your best life. Healing is a bit like unconditional love. It surrounds you until you get what you need, and then it loves you even more. That's what wholeness looks like. Nothing missing, nothing broken. Life is good.

Take a moment. Sit quietly and breathe. Reflect on that for a while. Give your pain to God. What else are you going to do with it? You don't need to know exactly how to let it go - just surrender. Say, "Lord

Jesus, I'm not quite sure how to do this, but I need You."

Prayer of Surrender:

Lord, I give everything to You. Please heal me everywhere I hurt. Heal my family, Lord. I love them, and they need You too. Thank You for being who You are in our lives. I give it all to You right now, in Jesus' name, Amen.

Now take a deep breath. Relax. It's going to be alright. Even if things don't turn out the way you want them to, remember that God is still there. It will get better. Just trust Him.

CHAPTER 7
Forever Grateful

If you can't think of anything or anyone to be thankful for, just look around. Thank God for the smallest of things and have a thankful heart. Always be grateful for Him. Let Him heal you. Let the healing balm of His love reach deep into your soul, into those places where you allow no one else to go - the places in your heart where it's invitation-only. Yes, let Him in there. You know the place I'm talking about. Take a moment…think about it.

Stretch yourself to grow to the next level. Don't look back. Sometimes it's not good to dwell on the past, especially if God has brought you out of something and into something better. It might not be exactly what you wanted, but it's better than where you were. Think about Lot's wife. She looked back, longing for the past, and it cost her everything. Don't give up. I'm cheering for you. It feels good to be victorious, and it is good to be free.

Grief: I can't tell you how to grieve because everyone is different. But I can tell you this, don't give up. Please, don't give up. There is hope, there is love, there are opportunities, there is freedom, and there is a life worth living again. Don't stay in the place of pain. I know it hurts - trust me, I know.

I've cried a million tears (there's even scripture about how God treasures our tears). I'm bearing my soul to you because, for years, I used to say, "One day, I'll have something to say." And now, this is it.

This wasn't easy to share, and it took me a long time to get here, but I want better for you. You don't have to let a decade pass before you start living again or rediscover who you are after life happens. Everyone has been touched by some kind of hurt. I'm here to tell you to let the scars heal. Stop nursing the wound - let Jesus' love heal you. His love is the only thing infinite enough to penetrate that place no one else has access to. I call it the sacred place of pain. Most people have one, even if no one else knows it exists. If you don't have one, you're blessed, and I hope you know that and are thankful.

You are truly blessed if you've never had to cover your mouth as you sobbed uncontrollably from the depth of your soul. I'm writing this with a box of Kleenex beside me, but not from a place of bondage - from a place of peace. As my tears fall, I'm allowing our loving Heavenly Father, Jesus Christ, to continue to love me into that place of wholeness. I am now free. It's been a journey, but I hope my journey helps you with yours. Be encouraged. I promise, it's worth every tear you shed. And God does not forget your labor of love. He won't forget all of the things you did for someone else, even if they didn't deserve it. That's the hard stuff! All is well.

Amazement: Sometimes I look out at the trees and watch the birds. I'm so in love with everything God created, especially after the rain. I'm happy to be alive and in my right mind. There was a time when I thought I was losing it, but here I am. Trauma can make you feel that way. You will get through it too. Don't give up - there is more for you.

For those of you who have contemplated suicide, please don't. I know it seems like an escape, but I beg you—please don't. You are worth so much more than the pain you feel right now. God has an amazing plan for your life; that's why He created you, and He needs you. You have so much to offer, so please don't give up. Let Jesus into that secret place, and He will turn your darkness into light.

He heals the brokenhearted and binds up their wounds [healing their pain and comforting their

sorrow]. The Lord is close to the brokenhearted
and saves those who are crushed in spirit.
Psalm 147:3 AMP

I know what it's like to have a broken heart. Jesus is the only one who can heal emotional pain, and God is the only one who can restore your soul. That's why so many people turn to drugs or alcohol - to escape for just a moment. But it leads to even more problems. I believe that's why the scripture says Jesus came to heal the brokenhearted. He heals our physical pain, but He also heals our emotional wounds. When your soul is hurting, it's deep. And that's how people get caught up in those addictions - seeking temporary relief but at a great cost. They keep doing it, not realizing how deep they're falling. Then, they feel even worse. It's like a vicious cycle.

Take back your peace. Don't let anything disrupt your life. Even Jesus said, "Peace, be still." If life has left you finishing something alone and unplanned, it can feel overwhelming or maybe impossible. But find something healthy to take your mind off of it, even for just a moment. Sometimes, that little break is all you need to pull yourself out of the slump. I don't want you to give up. Let's walk through this together. I'm reaching out to give you hope, to lead you to the Healer so that you can lead others. The Bible says that you are fearfully and wonderfully made (Psalm 139:14). God made you out of His love for you. You are part of a divine plan. Imagine that!

Now, let's talk about the spirit of procrastination. It's real. I look back and think about where I'd be if I had just taken a leap of faith sooner. But I also believe God is infinitely wise. He knew I would procrastinate, so He made provisions for my purpose. He factored in my shortcomings and imperfections. So, don't beat yourself up. The devil can't use that against you anymore, and I'm so incredibly grateful for that in His love for me and you, He took care of that too!

Before He formed you, He knew you.
Where we are weak, He is strong.
We can't do anything without Him.
We need Him, and He needs us.
Together, we are one.

Prayer of Trust

Lord Jesus, please help us to trust You and not procrastinate, delaying our destiny. We surrender to You, and we choose to trust You instead of relying on our own understanding. Thank You for all You've done for us. We honor You and are forever grateful. In Jesus' name, Amen!

CHAPTER 8

At the Point of Exhaustion

We all get tired sometimes - especially when we're faced with constant trouble or trauma. It's a whole different level of exhaustion when it feels like one thing after another keeps piling up. You feel overwhelmed and discouraged because it seems like it will never end. Before you can even resolve one issue, here comes another. The weight can be unbearable, especially when everyone around you - your family, children, or even your parents - needs something from you during the storm, and you can't seem to find a way out. It can feel like you're drowning.

Occasionally, the people closest to us are the ones causing the most grief. I've often wondered why. Why would someone make my life, or our lives, more difficult? Why do people who are hurting lash out at the ones trying to help them? That's where the frustration sets in - when you try to make sense of it.

True love, however, means staying kind even when someone has done everything to hurt you. That takes strength. It can take everything you've got to do the right thing, even when wrong is being done to you. Our natural instinct is to fight back, but if

50

you're trying to set an example - especially for your children, as I was, it requires humility. So, I humbled myself before the Lord and chose to love anyway. Even though I thought it would kill me.

It's extremely hard to continue being kind when, no matter what you do, it's never enough. They might even resent you, as strange as that seems. Yet, despite the mistreatment and betrayal, I remained faithful. It was NOT easy by any means, but I wanted my children to learn something different. I wanted peace in our home, and it had to come through me.

There were many times I wanted to quit and walk away, but I stayed. My situation was delicate, and it required a tremendous amount of patience and hope. I prayed and asked God to help my doubts even as I struggled with my faith. What I mean is I knew God's word; I trust Him. But it took a long time to see the results. Although I believed God would fix things somehow, I was struggling to keep my faith.

Hope postponed grieves the heart: but when a dream comes true, life is full and sweet.
Proverbs 13:12 The Voice

Yes, it hurts to keep caring when you're being mistreated. And it hurts even more to say "I'm sorry" when you know you're not wrong. But there comes a point when you must set boundaries. You can't continue allowing people to mistreat and manipulate you. Often, they take out their anger on you because you're there. And you become the one who has to pay the price. Other cases could be they're angry because they have an illness and might not realize it. Mental illness is real too, but it doesn't mean you have to endure it. Get help when it's needed.

In my situation, I believe it was a combination of misplaced anger and illness. I often asked, "Why me, Lord? What did I do to deserve this?" I used to wonder if I had done something wrong, but then I began to realize something: just as the devil uses people to hurt others, God uses people to love others. Sometimes, He chooses those of us who are strong enough to handle the burden, even when we think we can't.

We also have to be willing; the Father is gentle. Although He chooses us, He still lets us choose to be a part of His divine plan.

If He didn't choose the right person, the mission wouldn't get accomplished. He knew we could be trusted with it, even if it didn't feel like it at the time. God couldn't pick someone full of anger or hate - that would have only made things worse. He needed someone willing to show love and patience. He needed someone who was willing, like us.

I know it's unfair and there were many SO many times I wanted to defend myself. I asked myself, why am I allowing this type of abuse or mistreatment? But I had to trust that God would make things right. I mean I had to dig deep in my soul to remain godly. I've heard that God will use you for someone else's benefit, and neither of you can see it yet. But, trust that God has a purpose.

Now, let me be clear - you should never stay in a situation just because of your children. Trust me, they know what's going on. You can't hide it from them. And if the situation is dangerous - if there's physical, emotional, or mental abuse - you must prioritize safety and seek help. Pray about it, and don't be afraid to do what you need to do to be safe. Hopefully, your situation will get better and restoration can take place. My situation didn't resolve the way I had hoped, and we were heartbroken over it. However, we were able to walk through the healing process as a family. We're still walking that path every day, and it's a lot better.

Looking back, I used to think I was weak and my oldest son thought I was too. I felt like I was letting the enemy win because I was so unhappy and things were not getting better at all. But I'm glad I didn't give up. I'm glad my husband knew that we loved him in spite of the hurt. Still, you have to know when it's time to walk away - when things are too toxic, and loving from a distance is the best choice.

The truth is, you can't help who you love, and while you can't control their behavior, you can control yours. Life has a way of catching up, and God has a way of making things right. It's a new season now, a new time in our lives. And when you finally make it through the hurt, brokenness, and betrayal, it will be so worth it.

I'm glad to say that I can smile again - without the weight of brokenness on the inside. I stayed faithful, even when it nearly broke me and, in the end, we got the victory. It doesn't always look the way you think it will – it may take you looking back once you're out of it to see it. But trust me - God is with you through it all. Remember, sometimes you lose a battle, but you win the war. Stay faithful to God, and He will see you through everything. I promise.

CHAPTER 9
Decisions:
The Power of Choice

A lot of decisions that we make are attached to an emotion. If you haven't dealt with past hurts or trauma, your ability to see clearly can be impaired or your vision can become cloudy. Either way, unhealed areas can affect the quality of our decision-making. Remember, every decision has a consequence, whether good or bad. Don't allow negative experiences to prevent you from moving forward and making quality decisions for your life. You can choose healing! You can choose hope! You can choose to believe that God has better for you! Your thoughts are always present, and that's why the Bible says, "As a man thinks, so is he." Everything in life comes down to a decision; that's the power of choice.

Even when we encounter things that are beyond our control, we can still choose how we respond, act, behave, believe, and do. Remember, the Gentile woman who Jesus called a dog? Instead of getting upset at His remarks, she chose to answer in faith, "Master, even the dogs eat the crumbs that fall from their master's table" (Mt. 15:27). She understood Jesus' analogy and didn't take it personally. She was on a mission and as a result of her faith, Jesus healed her daughter. How are you responding to life? Are you still walking around with unhealed hurts and unresolved issues? Give it to Jesus. Respond in faith to His Word and allow Him to heal those areas, so you can fulfill your mission. I know it may sound too good to be true, but it really does start with a decision.

When you go through difficult times and emerge on the other side, you may not be the same person you were when you entered that trial. I know I'm not the same person - it changed me. I allowed the Lord to transform me for the better. It wasn't easy, but you have to decide whether you want to be bitter or better.

I remember one day the Lord spoke to me through a minister, saying, "Janice, you can be pitiful or powerful, but you can't be both." Gut-wrenching pain makes you want to run away from it - anything to escape. But you can't drink it away, smoke it away, snort it away, or sex it away. You can be as hateful as you want toward others, but that won't help you either. We all have a God-shaped hole in us, and only He can fill it. Allow Him to fill it. Yes, you can hurt on your way to recovery, but it's part of the process.

CHAPTER 10
A Mother's Love

How do I describe the love of a mother? I don't think there are words in the English language that truly capture the level of desperation and satisfaction that comes with that title. As I reflect, I ask myself, "How do I express this and stay positive?" The immense anguish I felt made me more committed to winning. I was determined to live because I wanted to see my children grow up. It took everything in me - all of my strength - to get back up after life knocked me down - the antagonism, deceit, manipulation, and betrayal were almost unbearable.

I love my sons deeply. I've always tried to protect them from anything or anyone that might cause them harm. Yes, I'm a mother bear. There's nothing I wouldn't do for them. I sacrificed to give them a good education, something both their father and I wanted for them. I know I made mistakes, but they knew I loved them dearly. Every drop of blood, sweat, and tears was not in vain. Today, we are very close, and we love each other without measure.

That makes me think about how much more God loves us. If I can love my sons like that, how much more does He love us? That kind of love must come from Him - the kind of love that flows naturally, without any effort. It's just there. I had to keep going for them because they needed me, and I needed them. My love for them pushed me to keep pressing on. I wouldn't dare quit. Those are my babies, and we were in this together. No matter how traumatic it got, I couldn't give up.

We faced the future together, not fully knowing what life would look like without their father. It felt like I had to swallow the biggest pill lodged in my throat, wipe away the tears, and move on. Along the way, I had to forgive a lot of people. They didn't make it easy, and grieving at the same time made it almost unendurable. The pain was excruciating.

Remember when I talked about closure and how sometimes you don't get it? That's exactly what I mean. You just keep going because you don't have a choice. What's done is done. Sometimes, other people take away your choices, and you have to hold on to what little you have to get through the next part of life - one moment, one day at a time.

I had to make sure my heart stayed right with the Lord, because I knew I couldn't walk this journey without Him. I constantly checked myself while struggling to forgive. Some people didn't understand why I didn't fight back. Believe me, I wanted to so bad and some other people wanted to fight for and with me too. But I needed God to fight for me more. So, I stayed out of it and asked them to do the same. It took every fiber of my being to hold back, but I knew God could do far more for me and my sons than I ever could. In my heart, I felt they didn't deserve forgiveness, and I didn't want to pray for them. And I didn't, not for a very long time.

I'm not ashamed to admit that I felt justified in not letting them off the hook. In my heart, what they did was unforgivable! It was like scrambled eggs - it couldn't be undone. The short version is this: we held two separate memorial services. My sons, my family, and our friends held one, and their father's family held another, but with him (their father). He was cremated, and our thoughts and feelings were completely disregarded. We had no voice because it was taken away from us. To this day, my sons don't have a place to lay flowers in remembrance of their father. This was our non-closure.

Over time, I've grown. I can now pray for those who hurt us, though it took me a while. I'm not completely healed, but I'm better - much better. The hardest part was not being able to say goodbye the way we thought we would. That was the crushing agonizing heartache that ruled my soul until I finished writing this book.

I think about the story of Jonah and the whale. Like Jonah, I felt the people who hurt us didn't deserve forgiveness. It's easy to feel this way about others, but we don't always apply the same standards to ourselves. Now, I'm ready to reclaim my life. Everything I didn't get to do before, I will do. Seeing my sons live free from past trauma brings me peace, but the only way to truly have a new beginning is through forgiveness. You have to forgive.

Trusting God to forgive myself and those who hurt us is the only path to real healing. God is so good, even when we don't deserve it. His goodness overtakes us and blesses us in ways we can't even comprehend. Think about that for a moment - He loves us without measure, and He deserves our praise. I am nothing without Him.

That's why I decided to step back and let God lead me because I can't live without Him. He's my life, and I live and breathe because of His faithfulness. Sometimes, I feel His presence deep within my soul, and I'm so honored to belong to Him. When you know His love, you begin to worship, and nothing else matters. It's just you and Him. It's truly a relationship. I ask Him about everything because I really want to know what He thinks. I am forever grateful! There's so much in Him that can't be compared to anything or anyone else. He's the beginning and the end.

I'm still amazed when I look back and see how far He's brought me. There's no other reason to look back except to reflect on what He's already done for you. His love never stops; it's a continual flow that can never be clogged. No matter what you've done or didn't do, He's still there. So you see, He accounted for it all. He covered everything, my friend. Forgive yourself. He'll help you with that too.

Circle of Pain, Cycle of Hurt

It's hard to watch someone you love become someone else and take their pain out on you. You've probably heard that "hurt people hurt others." It's true and it's a vicious cycle. That's why I'm writing this - to help you break free from whatever is holding you back. No matter what it is, you can be free.

We must stop the cycle of hurt and begin the healing process. We're already bleeding, so let's give purpose to our pain by surrendering to God's love and healing. It's not easy, standing in the aftermath, picking up what's left of our dream, relationship, marriage, home, or career. It might not seem like much, but you do have something left. Whether it's hope or the opportunity to rebuild, you can start again. If I can, anyone can.

That's what this book is about: starting over. Rebuilding with little or no hope, learning to begin again while you heal.

Pace yourself. We always want things to happen instantly, but they rarely do. And even if they did, we'd still have to go through the process. No matter how much we dread it, life is always happening, and there's nothing we can do about it. So, we might as well learn and grow through it. Don't rush. Learn to take each moment, each day, one at a time.

Write things down, get a plan, and work through it. Sometimes you'll have to adjust, and that's okay. Just keep working the plan, because there really is no alternative. Go ahead and start living well!

Now, let's talk about what other people think. Just kidding, let's not! I know it's hard because we all want to be liked, admired, accepted, loved, and appreciated. We love the accolades. But don't let that overshadow what God thinks of you. His opinion is what matters. Don't let other people's opinions determine whether you succeed or fail. You will be alright, trust me. God is way ahead of you, and your destiny isn't dependent on what others think, do, or say.

CHAPTER 11
The Pain of Forgiveness

What about the people who hurt us? Will they get what they deserve? And will we get what we deserve, too? Forgiveness is a complex thing. We all want justice for what's been done to us, but how often do we stop and think about the things we've done to others? It's important to remember that we all reap what we sow, in one way or another. Sometimes, we won't know or see if those who hurt us got what was coming to them. I often found myself asking, "Lord, what's happening here? I need to know they didn't completely get away with what they did to me!" I know we want to see it - I did too. But over time, compassion has filled my heart, and now I don't want to see them suffer. Imagine that!

But just because you don't see it doesn't mean it's not happening or hasn't already happened. Your focus should be on your relationship with the Lord and moving forward into the victory He has for you. Eventually, the pain will pass, and you won't even realize it after a while. Remember, this goes for us, too - something else to think about.

We all know that people are complicated. As shared in the previous chapter, "Hurt people hurt other people." At first, I didn't fully understand it because I didn't see myself as someone who could do that. If I did hurt others, it was never intentional. I'm talking about the kind of hurt that's manipulative and hateful on purpose. Sometimes, we need to have an honest conversation with ourselves and weigh the pain we carry. We have to decide whether to hold on to the pain or deal with it in order to move forward.

Some people prefer to stay in a painful situation because they're afraid of the unknown - they don't know what kind of new pain awaits, so they stick with what's familiar. But we must change.

You can't be the person you want to be and the person you are at the same time.

Just because you know better doesn't mean you'll do better.

Every once in a while, we have to be willing to endure temporary discomfort for lasting positive change. It's like exercising. It hurts and is difficult at first, but if you stick with it, you'll start to see progress. And that progress encourages you to keep going. The same is true for emotional pain. We must keep pushing ourselves toward wholeness, even if it means digging ourselves out of a dark place. It's like being trapped in a cave - you can't live there, so you must fight your way out to survive.

The question is, are you okay with staying where you are? Some people are content with mediocrity and not reaching their potential. Are you? They don't want to do the hard work it takes to get what they want or need. But it's up to us to make those tough decisions. It's a matter of following through with the choices we make for our own lives.

Think about it like this: you can choose the pain of recovery or the pain of staying the same. The pain is yours to choose, my friend! I say, let's choose the pain of growth and progress together. It's amazing how the Lord gently reveals things about ourselves that we didn't even know. For example, I hate injustice so much that I have to be careful not to hold grudges or let unforgiveness creep in. It's a fine line for me, and I often pray, Lord, please help me so I won't hinder my own life.

Back to how incredible it is to have compassion and love for someone who has mistreated you. That kind of love can only come from God. Life isn't always fair, but God is! He is just, and He will always make wrong things right if we handle the wrongs in the right way and trust Him. I've had to remind myself that God still has a good plan for my life and for my children's lives, even when forgiving someone feels brutal. You have to make it through the hard part to get to the good part.

I remember feeling so hurt by betrayal that I wanted to defend myself. I wanted God to clear my name because I didn't want people thinking I was a heartless person. That was another big hurdle for me, and it brought a tremendous amount of pain. God doesn't always give us all the answers, and that can feel unbearable. It felt so unfair, and I thought it would kill me if I didn't get justice.

The torment of trying to figure out why you were betrayed can be overwhelming. If you don't find the answers you're looking for, you'll only end up in confusion and frustration. Stop trying to figure it out. The only option is to trust Him. You have to let go of the need for explanations and trust that God will take care of it. I know - it's lousy – but it's the best way.

Forgiveness isn't just about releasing others - it's really about freeing yourself.

CHAPTER 12
Gut-Wrenching

One day, I received a call saying the absolute worst happened: William had passed away. I couldn't believe it. How was I supposed to tell our sons? Why didn't he get healed? Why didn't we get the miracle we had prayed for? I don't know. It's been 10 years now, and I still don't have the answer. But here's the peace I've found - I'm no longer trying to figure it out. The pain was so deep, so paralyzing, that I was in complete disbelief. I don't think I've ever felt so sick in my life.

The death of a loved one is gut-wrenching. It reaches into your soul, and nothing - not words, not comfort - makes it feel better. Your mind races with thoughts, wondering where they are spiritually. You don't have to worry if they are a believer, but if they weren't, you wonder. I think God knows why. He alone understands their personal hurts and traumas, just as He knows ours. In moments like this, you have to find the courage to rise up and do what must be done. There's no place to run, no retreat - you have to face one of life's most devastating pains.

That first step toward acceptance is the hardest. There's so much to do, and the reality of them no longer being alive is unbearable. My heart shattered into a million pieces that day. I questioned, "Where is God in all of this? Why won't He answer? Why can't I hear Him?" We had prayed so much for healing, but it didn't happen the way we wanted. Writing this chapter was the hardest for me. In fact, it's the last chapter I wrote. It still feels raw, and the tears fall so hard that I can barely see. My God was silent.

Deep Hurts: Some wounds require more than stitches. They need surgery, and Jesus is the surgeon. Our physical bodies can heal with stitches if it's just a flesh wound, but the deep wounds, they take more. Only Jesus can heal those. When surgery is required, it takes longer to heal, but the healing will come. We have to follow the doctor's orders to recover, and with the Lord, we must follow His word and trust that healing will come to pass. It's going to hurt either way, so you might as well hurt while you're healing. You must open your heart.

My Thoughts: I can't imagine how my sons must feel. I hurt for them, too. Sometimes, it's just too much. This was the "non-closure." Sometimes, closure isn't just about other people - it can be about

God, too - an unanswered prayer, not understanding something, feeling like your choices have been taken away, especially in moments like this. But eventually, you have to accept the loss you've just had or experienced and find the courage to move forward.

In this part of my journey, I've learned there are different levels of courage. You might have the courage to fight off a dog, but not the courage to face a snake. And then, there's the courage to move on with life. I had to find the strength to tell our sons, to plan a memorial without their father, and to finish raising them - all without the closure I so desperately needed.

Did I have the courage to lift my head and pay the price fear demanded in order for me to move forward into the unknown? This was something I had to do by myself. No one could walk with me. Somehow, I found the strength and took our sons with me. We only had each other, and I had Jesus. He was with me every step of the way. I just kept walking and never looked back.

The fear was overwhelming, and I didn't know what to say or do for them. They were my babies, and we walked through it together. We all grieved separately, but still together. It was one of the hardest things I've ever had to do. I think that's why, after all this time, it still hurts so much. I couldn't stop - I had to keep going, keep working, keep paying the bills, keep raising them. I didn't have time to sit with my pain and let life pass me by.

They needed me, and I needed them. We needed Jesus, and I'm so grateful that He never left me - even when it felt like I was alone. There was a quiet strength inside me that kept me grounded. That's the only way I can describe it. My love for my sons gave me the strength to keep going because I loved them with everything in me.

Losing William was the crescendo of my story. That stack of papers that were blown out of my hands, the ones that were never recovered was that love, and my life as I knew it then was changed. I'll forever miss him, and I will always love him.

CHAPTER 13
The Other Side

If someone asked me now how I would describe my life, I would say, "The rest of the papers that were blown and recovered is this book that you're reading right now." Now, we're on the other side of it all, and I can't help but think about the story of Shadrach, Meshach, and Abednego. They were obedient to God, but not without a cost. In the face of incredible pain and danger, they trusted in the Lord. When they refused to bow down to King Nebuchadnezzar, they were thrown into a furnace that was heated seven times hotter than usual. The fire was so intense that the soldiers who threw them in were consumed by the flames and died.

But then, something remarkable happened and King Nebuchadnezzar jumped to his feet in shock. Although, He had ordered three men into the furnace, there were four walking around inside, unharmed. He saw the Son of God in there with them. Jesus had joined them in the fire, and they were walking and talking as if nothing had happened. The king shouted for them to come out, amazed by what he had witnessed. He recognized that they served the Most High God.

The powerful part of the story is that when Shadrach, Meshach, and Abednego walked out of the furnace, they didn't even smell like smoke. That's me and my sons. God kept us through it all, and here we are on the other side, untouched by the fire that could have consumed us. We made it!

Now, as we look forward to our future, our faith is stronger than ever. We know how far we've come, and we are so thankful for God's love that surrounded us through the toughest time of our lives. Although I couldn't see it then, I can see it clearly now. The two loves - my love for my family and God's love for all of us - He was with us through it all.

Forgiveness is the key that helps us to get to the other side. It doesn't mean that what happened was okay. It doesn't erase the wrong. What it does is release you from being bound by the pain. It removes their power to control your emotions and, thus, your life. It allows you to move forward, to start over, and to rebuild. Without forgiveness, it's impossible to start fresh. Peter asked Jesus how many times shall he forgive his brother, seven times? Jesus tells Peter in Matthew 18:12, "I do not say to you, up to seven times, but up to seventy times seven."

To forgive "70 times 7" is a reminder that forgiveness is not a one-time act. It's a continual process, not only for others but also for ourselves. Forgiveness freed me from the pain of betrayal, heartache, and loss. It allowed me to walk through the fire and come out without the bitterness or anger that could have consumed me.

Jesus loves you SO MUCH, will you trust Him?

"For I know the plans I have for you," declares the Lord, "plans to prosper you and not to harm you, plans to give you hope and a future."
Jeremiah 29:11 NIV

CLOSING THOUGHTS
Author's Personal Note

Hi there,

I hope sharing my story encourages you to seek healing for yourself and those around you. The only way to truly achieve that is through a relationship with God. Jesus is the true healer, and He'll help you forgive, even when it's one of the hardest things you've ever had to do.

Father, I pray for everyone who has read this book. May it minister to their soul, and I speak peace over their lives. In Jesus' Name, Amen.

Love always,
Janice

Prayer of Salvation

The Bible says in John 3:16 KJV "For God so loved the world, that He gave his only begotten Son, that whosoever believeth in him should not perish, but have everlasting life." If you have not accepted Jesus Christ as the Lord of your life or if you have not invited Him into your heart as your personal Lord and Savior, please say this prayer out loud.

Lord Jesus, I come before You confessing that I'm a sinner. I believe that You are God's only begotten son who died on the cross, for me. I need you and I ask you to come into my heart. I make you my Lord and Savior. In Jesus Name, Amen.

Please continue to develop your relationship with the Lord. Talk to Him, just like I'm talking to you. Ask Him anything and trust that He will answer and show you.